Conflict Resolution in the Workplace

How to Handle and Resolve Conflict at Work

by Doug Wesley

Table of Contents

Introduction

When people hear the word "conflict" they tend to perceive an exaggerated example of it. The assumption is that conflict always takes the form of some physical or otherwise violent confrontation between groups of people (i.e. riots or war). It's also thought of as something that happens only in certain aspects of society, such as in politics or between rival ethnic groups. The thing is, conflict often arises from seemingly unimportant, microscopic issues, and most of the time, it's entirely unintentional. In fact, most conflict arises from mistakes, inadvertence, or even misunderstanding. But conflict is everywhere, and it takes on many forms. In a world with so many people – each with their own opinions, experiences, and interests to look after – it's simply impossible for everyone to always agree. Conflict is inevitable.

Since it's simply not possible to avoid conflict altogether, then the best alternative is to learn to deal with it in the best way possible by developing the skills required to resolve conflict quickly and effectively. Without these skills, conflict will only fester and escalate, causing even more problems to the growing number of parties within its wake.

Now let's be honest, conflict resolution isn't always easy. If it was easy, then everyone would be capable of it, and we wouldn't experience the type of damage it can do to a person, a company or institution, or even a country or continent.

But nonetheless, once developed, conflict resolution is a great skill to have. This book is going to focus specifically on conflict resolution in the workplace. Stress arising from conflict with coworkers or other office personnel is not only damaging to the people directly involved, but it comes with an inherent adverse impact to the company as a whole, exhibited through an unpleasant work environment and a decrease in productivity. The good news is, through better understanding and a little strategy; workplace conflict can be more easily avoided and resolved. Throughout this book, I'm going to show you how to mediate conflicts and arrive at amicable solutions acceptable to all parties. More importantly, you will learn how to conflict-proof your workplace to prevent conflicts before they have a chance to get out of hand. If you are ready to take the first step to creating a stress-free and productive workplace, then let's get started!

Chapter 1: Conflict in the Workplace

There is perhaps no more common place for conflict to brew and be felt than the workplace. Unlike other social circles where people come together because of things they agree on, institutions like the office are composed of people who need to be there regardless of their differences. And more often than not, members of the workplace have to get along with each other in order to meet their common goals.

In order to be productive, the workplace, and its people, must work in harmony. Anything that disrupts or could potentially disrupt any work-related relationship could damage the system. At some point in our lives we've worked with someone we'd rather not, and that affects many things. Bosses can become less objective, employees can be distracting, and co-workers can be less cooperative. None of that is ever good.

It's Just Work. Why Should I Care?

The common misconception is that conflict resolution is the sole task of the head of human resources or someone with a managerial position. That's not always the case.

While it's logical for those higher up to lead the resolution of conflicts, everyone who functions within the same environment should be concerned. You don't even have to be a direct party of the conflict to know that trouble can affect you.

Imagine working on your own desk where you witness existing tension between two co-workers. You don't even have to know their names - they could come from an entirely different department. You just have to happen to see them in that state. Whether you are aware of it or not, this sort of thing affects you as well.

And yes, it does get worse. Consider the following:

- Conflicts are a source of unnecessary stress. They break people's focus from what they should be concentrating on instead. The distraction is even more potent when the tensions are subtle because the affected parties have no outlet.

- Conflicts cause work groups to fall apart. Teamwork is almost always a must in a workplace, and misunderstandings within the ranks could affect the entire team. This makes the group less productive, if not really destructive.

- Conflicts are a terrible strain on resources. Whether we're talking about the company's resources or that of the individual employees; whether they are tangible resources like capital or intangible resources like time and energy, conflicts are just a waste of so many things. People could just jump ship if the stress is too much to handle, and that could happen in the worst moments.

- Conflicts also bleed out of the office. When they escalate, parties take the issue very personally and the family and friends of these workers start to see how much of a toll their work is taking on them.

So whether you're a manager who is mediating the conflict or a bystander who hears the gossip around the office, you are just as much a stakeholder to conflict resolution as any party to it, not because you have a direct interest in an existing conflict, but rather because you, and everyone else, has an interest in maintaining a conflict-free work environment.

Moreover, conflict resolution is a joint effort. Since resolving and preventing conflicts entail a system, it is ideal that everyone who takes part in that system is aware of how things are done.

Conflict resolution, therefore, is something everyone should learn to do. This will guarantee that knowledge of grievance machineries, preventive measures, and other mechanisms that are designed to minimize workplace conflict is sustained and made available to everyone. Knowledge, as the old saying goes, is power.

More than resolving conflicts, this guide will look into creating a work environment that is capable of addressing conflicts when they inevitably arise. This includes:

- Understanding what a conflict-resilient workplace looks like

- Being familiar with common types of conflict and knowing how to deal with them

- Creating a system for addressing conflict as they arise

- Do's and don'ts during conflict.

This guide will make use of general conflict resolution principles and apply them directly to the workplace scenario in the hopes that it equips all parties who have an interest in a conflict-free environment.

Chapter 2: Creating a Conflict Resilient Workplace

Visualization is the first step to building a conflict resilient workplace. You need to know what your workplace ought to look like if it is to withstand any conflicts that may arise.

Conflict Resilient Workplaces Start with Communication and Relationships

First and foremost, a conflict resilient workplace will always focus on improving communication and building relationships. This is for the obvious reason that all conflicts arise from the lack of these two important things. Misunderstandings arise out of failure to communicate properly, while more direct conflicts are a result of a lack of mutual respect.

You want your workplace to be conducive for developing these two things. Failing to understand that from the very beginning will result in failure of the conflict resolution system at its onset.

Conflict Resilient Workplaces Prepare for All Stages of Conflict

There are basically three stages of conflict, represented by the very simple timeline: before they happen, during times they are likely to happen, and when they do happen.

A relatively peaceful workplace will make it a point to prepare for all these stages such that everyone knows what to do as the need arises. Ideally, you should strive to prevent all possible conflict - there's no point in waiting for them to get worse before doing anything about them. But because these things can inevitably escalate for many reasons, everyone must also know how to tell what stage of the conflict they are in and what to do at that stage.

This knowledge includes the logistical and systematic aspects of conflict resolution (i.e. where to go and who to talk to in case the conflict escalates).

Being caught off guard when the conflict escalates will put people in a situation that's no different from being unprepared and, naturally, invite failure.

Conflict resolution systems vary between institutions, but the stages are more or less the same:

- The **preventive stage** is where most establishments should focus on. Preventing conflicts is the least costly way of ensuring a conflict resilient workplace. This is where the establishment takes measures to enhance the relations among co-workers as well as ensure that everyone knows their boundaries through proper information and communication.

- The **collaborative stage** is the part where workers are actively working with each other in some activity, may it be short or long term. This is the time when the decisions and actions of all parties have to be kept in check so they don't cause conflict. This is also the time when people who could possibly be the source of conflict are confronted to prevent any trouble. Here, whether or not conflict will arise is dependent on how well everyone cooperates.

- The **resolution stage** starts from the time when differences become prevalent between parties until the point their issues are resolved. This usually requires the intervention of an authority, either through formal or informal procedures. This is likely to be the final part of a conflict and the point at which it must be resolved if permanent damage to everyone in the workplace is to be prevented.

Conflict Resilient Workplaces Are Context Sensitive

Oftentimes some workplace environments make the mistake of establishing certain protocols and services for the sake of making them. But when employees start to make use of them, it feels like nothing happens. In other words, management enforces these features simply out of formality and not really to genuinely serve its employees.

Every workplace has its own unique set of needs. As such, its services should be very specific to those needs, and the conflict resolution system is no different. What is well within the acceptable standards of one workplace will differ in others. The same thing goes for policy making (i.e. some offices require the use of uniforms while others are more relaxed about the dress code). What constitutes as acceptable practice or enforceable regulation will always differ between offices.

Resolving conflicts should be sensitive on both a macro and micro level. Meaning, management should be clear regarding the acceptable standards of behavior among its workers but at the same time, remain sensitive to exceptions.

Conflict Resilient Workplaces Are Compliant with Regulations

When policies are set, they must be followed. Failure to enforce them consistently and fairly will cause people to lose trust in that system, leading to failure and perhaps a permanent inability to address these concerns.

This aspect of a conflict resilient workplace is reliant on the enforcer's ability to uphold these policies, although it does require some cooperation on the part of the workers.

Whether or not other people cooperate, however, the system that has been built to address grievances as well as help prevent conflicts must be allowed to take its course in all cases.

Conflict Resilient Workplaces Are Evolving

Since no system is ever perfect, it's very important to acknowledge the fact that the conflict resolution model of any workplace would always be a work in progress. This is because the success of the model is hinged on its ability to address a wide variety of issues. Every time a conflict is dealt with successfully or otherwise, it is important for all parties to assess the overall performance of the system in the recent case.

An evolving conflict resolution model should also be able to assess the kinds of problems that it has to address using questions like:

- What was the cause of the problem? Was it avoidable?

- If the problem escalated, were there steps that could have been taken to stop it earlier on?

- What was the impact of the conflict in the workplace?

- What was the solution undertaken? Was it the best one, given the circumstances?

These kinds of questions and more can help the management understand the nature and gravity of the problems to be better equipped to deal with problems in the future. Undoubtedly, there will be areas for improvement, especially at the start.

Ideally, you will want to work towards creating an environment that promotes the abovementioned values insofar as conflict resolution is concerned. How you will achieve these goals will depend on your situation, but this guide can help you get there.

Chapter 3: The Evolving Conflict Resolution Model

Because conflict resolution models in the workplace are a work in progress, it is important to know the different steps to building this particular model. There are seven steps in total:

1. Establishing representation

2. Evaluating status quo

3. Identifying points for improvement

4. Formulating courses of action

5. Developing implementation plans

6. Implementation

7. Post implementation evaluation

Each step is a unique process that will require you to achieve short term goals in order to achieve the main goal of creating a system that is able to prevent as well as address conflicts.

Step 1: Establishing Representation. Conflict is prevented and resolved through proper communication and tolerance between various parties who have different viewpoints and needs. It is very important that the group directly working to develop the conflict resolution system includes representatives from all possible parties (i.e. rank-and-file employees, managerial employees, and the management). Remove a significant party and the conflict resolution system will be left disadvantaged. This could lead to failure of the system, and result in noncooperation.

Note: How complex the representative body is depends on the size of the workplace. If you're part of a small workplace, it's possible that a single person can be appointed to handle the entire task. What's important is that everyone's needs are factored into the system.

Step 2: Evaluating Status Quo. More often than not, you don't have to start from scratch when you're working to build a conflict resolution system. Even without one, people who have been working for some time unknowingly have a system of solving conflicts, only that it's not acknowledged and systematized. Maybe your office already has a person people turn to when there is a problem, or the co-workers already have an unspoken means of solving deadlocks in decision making.

Capitalizing on what the people in the workplace are familiar with could promote cooperation when solving conflicts.

In case there isn't an existing recognizable practice of resolving conflicts, then do a case study of the conflict culture in the workplace:

- What is the most common issue that the workplace often experiences?

- Are there complaints of dissatisfaction?

- How are these concerns being addressed, if at all?

During this step, the goal of the team is to develop a series of recommendations that need to be worked on. This is where, using the principles discussed in the previous chapter, you will build a conflict resiliency that's unique to your workplace.

Tip: Be very objective when assessing the status quo. Always look for evidence to prove existing problems that could otherwise be imagined or exaggerated because you will want to address real problems.

Step 3: Identifying Points for Improvement. This step sounds pretty much like the previous one, and that's because they go hand in hand. Once the recommendations are set, you need to identify how these recommendations are steered towards the goals of the workplace. During this step, you can:

- Make a checklist of these points for improvement

- Discuss which points should be prioritized

- Identify who is responsible for which aspect of improvement in the system

Step 4: Formulate Courses of Action. There are many ways to achieve a single goal, and this step focuses on how to pick the best course of action to take. There will naturally be one solution that's better than all others. Consider the following factors when deciding the best choice:

- Which option will best cater to the needs of all parties?

- Which course of action is the most cost-efficient (i.e. costs less but achieves the same optimum result)

- Which one is easier to sustain in the long term?

Tip: Try making a list of all options in one column and jot down their pros and cons. This always helps break the ties between seemingly equal options.

Step 5: Develop Implementation Plans. Once discussions are finalized and options have been affirmed, it's time to lay down the details for carrying out these chosen courses of action. Make sure to identify the following:

1. Person or persons tasked to implement the plan

2. Timeline for the task: including milestones and deadlines

3. Working budget

4. Consultation: who are the people whose cooperation is needed?

Make sure to leave allowances for these details. Not all plans go smoothly - some timelines may be delayed and costs increased. Make room for the unexpected.

Step 6: Implementation. This stage is quite self-explanatory. Just make sure that the person tasked to implement the proposed changes follows the plan as much as possible.

Step 7: Post Implementation Evaluation. Think of this as a post-test in comparison to Step 2. Simply assess the post-implementation scenario using the following guide questions:

- Were the set goals achieved?

- Were the identified problems and points for improvement solved or complied with?

- What were the specific problems encountered along the way? How were they addressed?

- How can the new system be further improved?

At this point, the cycle starts over again. As long as the conflict resolution model runs, there will always be room for improvement, which will call for further planning and implementation as time goes by.

Chapter 4: Common Types of Workplace Conflict

There are different kinds of workplace conflict, but there are general classifications. The classifications below are not all inclusive, as conflicts really vary from case to case. You may have already experienced or witnessed these in one form or another.

Discrimination

While the workplace is structured by ranks, the equality of all workers of the same ranks should remain a non-negotiable value. But the fact remains that there are people who end up being unfairly classified in the workplace, largely due to their ethnicity or gender. This comes in many forms, such as:

- Being given less or more portions of a group task, where everyone is expected to contribute equally;

- Being directly or indirectly excluded by colleagues from activities related to the company within the confines of the work place; or

- Getting fewer benefits than others who render equal work.

Cases of discrimination within the workplace make a long and possibly endless list, since there are simply so many ways to exclude a person unreasonably. Sometimes these are hard to spot, either because the person doesn't know he or she is being treated unfairly, merely tolerates the treatment, or doesn't have an avenue to voice the concern.

While there are cases of discrimination that escalate to mediation, most of this sort of conflict is best dealt with using preventive measures. Oftentimes, the establishment need not look beyond the laws within their jurisdiction to know what is considered a discriminatory practice. Beyond that, the management can impose clear guidelines to promote equal treatment among workers within the office.

Leadership Conflicts

Sometimes leaders don't always make the most popular decisions. When working with a team, it is expected that a subordinate will speak up to question the superior's judgment or even his or her authority.

What makes this kind of conflict tricky is that sometimes the subordinate is correct in pointing out the leader's mistake. On one hand, protocol will insist that the leader gets to have the final say. On the other, the leader could be making a mistake that would result in the failure of the entire team.

Again, a clear delineation as to who gets to decide what will prevent this sort of thing from escalating unnecessarily. Management must take care, however, not to dismiss the concerns of their subordinates as they, too, have an interest in seeing to it that the team succeeds in whatever projects it is undertaking.

Large scale leadership conflicts happen between a majority of the workers and the members of the board or the owner of the company. This is where strikes or lockouts can potentially happen.

Regardless of size, there is often legal and informal machinery to help parties negotiate their concerns. These problems are usually resolved by coming up with a compromise between both parties.

Personal Conflicts

As much as bosses would like to stay out of their employee's lives outside the workplace, employees have a knack of bringing their personal differences into the office. This, of course, comes in countless forms, but it calls for two general types of approaches.

First, if the personal conflict between the co-workers is a result of activities within the workplace (i.e. office gossip or bullying), it is best to step in and address the misconduct because the conflict is directly work-related.

But if the conflict stems from something that has nothing to do with work at all, it is often better for management to step back and simply intervene when the tension already affects others within the workplace. Businesses must be careful not to extend authority outside the office.

Like most personal conflicts, they can be resolved through proper mediation by a person both parties trust. More often than not, these misunderstandings can be discussed in a peaceful way. In case of irreconcilable differences, co-workers should at least be told to set their differences aside during work.

Responsibility Conflicts

When something goes wrong at work, confusion happens and conflict arises. Issues about who was supposed to do what and who caused which mistake start to arise. People start to play the blame game and nobody wants to take responsibility for anything bad that happens for fear of the consequences.

Sometimes co-workers don't take criticism very well, even from higher authorities, and this could escalate to personal conflicts or discrimination.

Conflicts like these arise from a general failure or misallocation of responsibility or work load. As such, it can only be resolved by setting clear parameters of responsibilities among co-workers and laying down standards that everyone must adhere to.

There are so many other types of workplace conflicts, but one thing that they all have in common is that they can be prevented or addressed through a conflict resolution system.

Chapter 5: Conflict Resolution from a Personal Perspective

Whether or not there is a conflict resolution model where you work, expect that conflicts will happen and you will need to know how to behave in these circumstances to help resolve it or, at the very least, not make it worse. Here are some tips to remember:

Set clear standards of behavior. Many personal conflicts happen because people think what they are doing is okay. By understanding what everyone within the workplace considers acceptable and unacceptable conduct, people are better able to keep themselves in line, significantly reducing possibilities of conflict.

A set code of conduct is useful for both interpersonal relations between co-workers as well as for work ethic.

Listen. Much of conflict comes from people not being able to get their sentiments across. When people are ignored or their needs are not met, they become frustrated and end up escalating a concern to a higher management level when it could have otherwise been dealt with easily.

Your boss and co-workers are people too, and they all have different needs. While management can't always solve every individual worker's problems, it should make a point of

35

creating a work environment where people's individual concerns are at least heard, so that they can be discussed.

Choose which conflicts to face and which to ignore. Depending on the nature of the conflict, facing a problem head on could alleviate the tension or make things worse. The question is, how do you tell which one is which? There are a series of tests that you can use to help make that call.

The first test is called the "right person test". Ask yourself if you are in the position to address the problem. If a person who works for you raises a concern against a fellow manager, it's better for you to refer him or her to the right official who can handle these complaints. If you are the project head of a team and one of your team members raises a concern, make sure you deal with it because it's your job.

Sometimes we can't help but get involved in other peoples issues, but dipping your fingers where they shouldn't be can only escalate conflict.

The second test is called the "what's in it for me" test. Take note that not all conflicts directly affect the workplace. Some co-workers may not see eye-to-eye but their disagreements are at best noticeable. If you don't think the conflict between two people can have any impact in the workplace, then it's advisable not to give it any attention. But if the conflict affects you or your workmates in some significant way, then maybe you should intervene.

The last test is the "worth" test. Simply ask yourself: is becoming involved in the issue worth it? Sometimes people engage in conflict for very petty reasons, and the best way to deal with it is to take the high road and just let it go. You don't always have to get into conflict for the sake of it. The conflict resolution system is there to alleviate stress from conflict, not aggravate it.

These tips apply to anyone who is faced with a conflict situation in the workplace - leader or member, manager or worker.

Chapter 6: Actions to Avoid during Conflict

Here are some things that you definitely should NOT do when you're in the midst of conflict.

Don't be afraid of conflict. You need to be aware of the reality that conflict naturally happens everywhere, and the worst place to be is in the dark - don't be caught off guard because you assumed everything would be perfect every day.

When you are faced with a situation, know that you have an establishment that is able to back you up. And yes, it will be a stressful process, but giving in to the fear will only cloud your judgment further.

By treating conflict resolution as something that's just part of the job, you are able to embrace it as part of your day-to-day responsibilities, allowing yourself to take control.

Don't let emotions rule your judgment. It's important not to get carried away. More often than not, how you react initially to a possible conflict scenario will decide whether or not there will be conflict to begin with. Thus, when something alarms you or makes you angry, make it a habit to hold your tongue, take a step back, and think about what you'll say next.

Don't take sides. No matter how much you agree with one party to a conflict, you should always remain impartial. That is the only way to make sure both parties will trust your advice when they bring the issue to you.

Taking sides will only make one party feel oppressed, causing him or her to become more aggressive or to feel rejected and oppressed. Either way, the conflict will inevitably escalate.

When you maintain a neutral position, both parties are more likely to listen to your reason than they would if they perceived you to be biased. It's important to consistently reassure everyone that you have their best interest at heart.

Don't blame others. There is a difference between understanding what caused the problem and throwing the blame to others. It is always better to see success and failure as owned by everyone rather than someone. That way, it will be easier to bear, especially by the person directly at fault.

In fact, having a circle of co-workers who recognize collective success and failures make an environment where it is easier for an individual to own up to his or her own mistakes.

So even if you know who exactly is at fault, don't give in to the knee-jerk reaction of pointing fingers. It doesn't help, except to make the situation worse.

On another note, if you know you are at fault, you're better off admitting to it. People will like you for that.

Don't believe everyone outright. One common cause of conflict is people reacting to things that have no basis (i.e. gossip, accusations). While it is important to trust the people you work with, you always have to take most accusations and concerns with a grain of salt. This will not only preserve your own integrity, but it will also help you manage your emotions before dealing with the issue if indeed it is legitimate.

Don't get too attached to conflict. This is important especially if the conflict is isolated at work. Leave your work at the office and don't let it bother you when you get home. That doesn't help solve the problem.

You should also learn to accept that not everything is under your control. Sometimes problems happen in the workplace simply because people weren't prepared for it. Some people are also just difficult to work with.

Not all conflict can be prevented or resolved fully. What you need to do in these situations is to just accept what you can't change and go back to work.

Conclusion

Learning how to deal with conflict in the workplace is indeed a life skill that everyone should learn, no matter where you work or what your position is. This is how successful people guarantee that everyone focuses on the goals of the workplace and stays productive despite individual disagreements.

Conflict resolution is not a one-man thing. It requires everyone's cooperation, and relies on open communication and good relations between co-workers. It requires a good conflict resolution model that is tailored to fit the context and needs of the specific workplace.

Conflict is inevitable, but that doesn't mean that we have to let it get the best of us. We have to be ready when it happens so we stay in charge of our emotions and outcomes and, naturally, our lives. After all, staying in control of the situations in our lives - including where we work - is one of the keys to success.

Finally, I'd like to thank you for purchasing this book! If you found it helpful, I'd greatly appreciate it if you'd take a moment to leave a review on Amazon. Thank you!

25001580R00028

Printed in Great Britain
by Amazon